If God Is Good,

Why Is There So Much Suffering and Pain?

Harold R. Eberle

WORLDCAST PUBLISHING
YAKIMA, WASHINGTON

If God is Good,
Why Is There So Much Suffering and Pain?

First Printing June 2003

Worldcast Publishing
P.O. Box 10653, Yakima, WA 98909-1653, USA
(509) 248-5837
www.worldcastpublishing
office@worldcastpublishing.com

ISBN 1-882523-24-5

Cover by Paul Jones
Cover Photo: Doug and Linda Arenson,
with background and setting by Bob Bartow

Printed in the United States of America

Thanks and Dedication

James Bryson reworks my words to flow smoothly and touch the hearts of my readers. He also added significant portions to the beginning and ending of this book. Pastors Charles and Joyce Sibthorpe offered helpful suggestions, and Sherrie St. Hillarie added a touch of class and grace. Jane Johnson is my secretary and administrative assistant, who can do all things well. Annette Bradley is my final editor and she is the expert with an eye for detail. My wife, Linda Eberle, keeps me on track in my writing and all areas of life. To these I owe a great deal of thanks for their help in completing this book.

I dedicate this work to my mother-in-law, who is now healthy and happy in the arms of the Lord, and to all the suffering people in this life who someday will be with her.

Table of Contents

Introduction

If you are reading this book, chances are that you have experienced pain. You may be suffering now; you may know someone who is suffering. You may have exhausted all possibilities, explored all avenues for relief, begged God until you have doubted His ability or even His existence.

Still, I want to offer you something that can help. It is not a cure, and it might not bring immediate relief, but it can put your soul at ease. It will give you comfort, strength, and hope.

Pearl, my wife's mother, was in pain—for more than 30 years. Arthritis ravaged her body, curled her fingers, and left her lying immobile in bed. Thin skin hung loosely on aching bones. Her husband, my father-in-law, faithfully provided for her, but they slept in separate bedrooms for three decades. She was alone in her pain. During the last two years of her life, Pearl stayed in a rest home near us. My wife spent precious time there everyday. By then Mom weighed less than 70 pounds. With every movement, her bones made cracking and grinding sounds. Only during the last few days of her life did her eyes cease crying out for help.

Pearl was God-fearing. When she was younger, she faithfully took her daughter (my wife) to church. I am glad she raised my wife in the way that she did. God was and is very important to both of them.

I don't know what Pearl thought about God during the last few years of her life. I was afraid to ask. It was painful to talk. Now I wish I'd had the courage to discuss with her some of the things I have learned since then—things I have written in this book.

Today, much of my work is in the poorer regions of Africa. I have seen tens of thousands of people living in garbage, with no jobs, no sewer system, and no clean water. Destitute children are everywhere—bare feet, open sores, sunken eyes. They live and die in those conditions.

Among other things, I teach them about God—how good He is.

In some cities in Africa, the orphan children who walk the streets carry small cups cut from the bottoms of plastic bottles. In the cups they put small amounts of glue, gasoline, or other toxins. The cups are held between their teeth to encompass their noses; they inhale the vapors constantly, keeping themselves in a state of stupor. I want to take them home, but the natives who live there warn me: "If you take them home, they will slit your throat at night!" Behind those glazed-over eyes are souls that never have been loved.

I have helped establish several orphanages in Africa, but the need is overwhelming, with hundreds of children being newly orphaned every day. War is a thief that takes parents away. AIDS leaves bodies where children find them. Other diseases move across the land as ripples across a pond.

Sometimes I cry. In spite of the pain, I still understand that God is good. In the following pages I will explain how that can be.

If your emotional wounds are fresh, then my answers may seem too simplistic, too calculated, for you to embrace at this time. If your heart is in anguish, then your head may not be ready to assemble thoughts that can make sense out of life. In that case, you need a hand to hold, seasons to pass, and a bird singing on your window sill. Although I cannot offer you those personal touches through these pages, I do desire to speak to your heart, in addition to your head. If I can help you calm the pain within, you may be able to grasp the ways of God—perhaps even know His presence in the midst of difficult times.

In my personal struggle, I did a lot of studying. In fact, I wrote another book, a more scholarly one, as I wrestled with the related questions and answers. That book is entitled, *Who Is God?* I recommend it for counselors, ministers, students of philosophy or theology, and leaders who must have a fuller understanding. The book you are holding is meant to help those who personally have faced pain and suffering, but now are ready to reassemble their thoughts, according to an anchoring belief that God is good.

Chapter 1
The Question

Where does suffering originate? The conventional wisdom holds that all things are based upon cause and effect. If you are similar to me, or the millions of others in Western society, your thinking runs along the lines of logical argument. If there is suffering, there is a cause. Find the cause and you can find a cure. Most of Western thought is based upon this cause-and-effect relationship.

This way of thinking has led to many great discoveries. Years ago, most diseases and calamities were attributed to supernatural powers, either evil forces or an angry God. But scientists, following the vein of logical, methodical exploration, have uncovered a more rational understanding of many of the afflictions that previously beset us. As a result, much of the suffering, which was common even 50 years ago, has been eradicated.

And yet suffering remains.

Medical doctors, researchers, psychologists, psychiatrists, and sociologists have uncovered dynamics to the human condition and have brought light and hope to millions.

And yet suffering remains.

There are accidents that take innocent people. There are diseases with no known cure. There are madness and acts of sheer cruelty that boggle the imagination. Our practical knowledge—while ever pressing into new frontiers—is limited.

There arises from our inner being, at the moment of greatest tragedy, a cry that is both universal and fundamental: "Why, God, why?" In this poignant moment, we find the question and the answer. The question is "Why?" and the answer is "God." And the final question remains: "Why?"

We make our appeal to a God Whom we consider good, One Who runs the universe and is aware of the very hairs on our head. We come—in that instant of naked supplication—to the Creator of the universe, that Author of all that we know or hope to find. And often the answer we receive is simply comfort, and sometimes understanding. But still the questions linger, and we may spend a lifetime wondering, "Why?" Why did a good God let this happen to me? Or to those I love? Or to those who did nothing to deserve it?

I want to explore this with you. Why is there so much suffering? Where did it originate? What do we do about it? Then I want to propose some answers to redirect your mind and heart to the only One Who can help.

Chapter 2
Hard Lessons of Life

Two friends have impacted my life from their wheelchairs.

The first was Danny, a fellow who grew up in the same neighborhood as I did. We had a unique bond because his birthday is the same as mine. As children we played ball together and we used to go swimming in the neighborhood pool. But as teenagers, Danny and I grew apart. He hung around the more popular students whereas I was more of a loner.

Then one day the news spread throughout school that Danny and another classmate, Phil, had been out drinking and that Phil drove his pickup truck off of a road down a steep embankment. Danny was thrown from the vehicle and left unconscious. In a panic, Phil pulled Danny to the top of the hill. To this day, no one knows for sure at what point Danny's spinal cord snapped, but he was left paralyzed from the waist down.

Danny's hospital stay and a long rehabilitation period removed him from the school environment. I lost touch with him.

Several years later, when I was attending a university, I walked into a restaurant/bar where Danny and Phil were drinking together. They were close. It was immediately evident that Phil was dedicated to his friend. He was faithful.

I never had talked to Danny since the accident. That day when I found myself standing in front of him, I was totally speechless. In my sheltered life, I had not been around handicapped people very much, and I was at a complete loss as to what to say. I did not know if I should express my sorrow, tell a joke, or pretend that nothing had changed.

When Phil saw me stumbling with my words, he realized that I was unable to treat Danny as a normal human being, that I couldn't see beyond his wheelchair. In reaction, Phil cursed at me. I suppose he did not want his friend to feel the shame of the moment. After an awkward greeting, I silently walked away feeling like an idiot.

Since that day, I have spent quite a bit of time with disabled individuals, and hopefully, I have learned a few things.

One friend stands out to me above all others. I did not meet Kyle until I was in my thirties. By then Kyle already had been confined to a wheelchair for several years. When I think about Kyle, I don't think about his wheelchair. I envision his smile, and I feel the encouragement that constantly flows from him to everyone around. Kyle is married to a woman who is equally as energetic, alive, and full of joy. Together they pastor a church. It is amazing what they have accomplished in life.

The first day I met Kyle, I asked him how he landed in his chair. As his wife drove us around town, Kyle explained how he was pouring his life into soccer, until one day on the field he landed on his neck, snapping his spinal cord. Even in the midst of his story, Kyle did not stop being positive. In fact, his voice filled the vehicle with energy and hope.

Later on, I asked Kyle when his accident happened. I thought he would continue in his jovial tone, but this question was different. He looked at me with a distant look in his eyes and said, "Eight years, four months, and three days ago." Silence froze the next moment. I don't remember what else we said that day, but I do remember that Kyle soon was refilling the vehicle with his energy and positive attitude.

These two friends have been a jolt to my comfortable world. We all live with unanswered questions. For the most part, we can ignore the resulting inner turmoil, yet when confronted by serious pain, injustice, death, or suffering, we do not know how to reconcile it with our belief—our hope—that God is good.

Chapter 3
Pain and Suffering Happen

One day Kyle, my friend who used to play soccer, explained to me how that right before his accident he had an impression that he was not supposed to go out onto the soccer field. He could not explain it, but he believes God was warning him that something tragic would happen. Kyle went out onto the field in spite of the warning.

If we believe that God truly was warning Kyle, then we may conclude that God did not want this tragedy to happen. Yet, it also is evident that God allowed Kyle the freedom to go out onto the field anyway.

Incidents like this help me understand God's involvement with this world. I am convinced that many things happen by chance, without God's direct control.

Look at Creation. It is beautiful—and dangerous. The ocean's waves roll in with hypnotic glory, but they also beat against the cliff's edge until the bank gives way, burying all in its path. The sun warms the Earth, but it also dries out the soil, leaving a desert waste. Waterfalls create breathtaking beauty, yet far downstream, floods come and destroy homes along with those who dwell therein. The wind blows, carrying seeds to fertile soil, but it also shakes a tree until a bird nest falls to the ground, killing newly hatched chicks.

Nature reveals a tremendous amount of randomness and chance.

Of course, there are natural laws governing all things—even how the wind blows and a bird's nest falls to the ground—but here I am referring to things which happen by chance in the sense of occurring without God's direct control.

Certainly, God can control anything He chooses. However, He also can allow many things in this world to proceed on their own according to natural processes.

One of my friends was crushed by a huge branch which broke free from a tree overhead. He was left handicapped and with severe headaches for years. I don't believe he deserved that. He wasn't any worse than anyone else. In fact, he lived as a God-fearing person. It happened not because God made the branch break, but because sometimes branches get old and gravity pulls them to the ground. Stuff like that happens on this planet.

Jesus talked about a comparable tragedy:

> *"Or do you suppose that those eighteen on whom the tower in Siloam fell and killed them, were worse culprits than all the men who live in Jerusalem? I tell you, no...."* (Luke 13:4-5a)

Jesus made it clear that this accident did not happen because those people were any more deserving of punishment than other people. It just happened. It could of happened to anyone.

Of course, God could have stopped that or any other tragedy from happening. He can do whatever He wants to do. However, He has chosen not to control everything.

Years ago, my wife created a story to help me understand a difficult situation which I was facing. She said a man walked up an old rotten set of stairs and one of the steps broke, causing the man to stumble and break his leg. She then asked me, "Did he break his leg because of God or the devil?" At the time, my mind was caught in the trap of thinking that either God or the devil was causing my problems. Looking me sternly in the eye, my sweetheart said, "He broke his leg because the step was rotten!" That helped me.

Bad things happen.

Chapter 4
God Is Not Controlling Everything

Whenever problems came my way I used to say, "God is in control." I don't say that anymore, because I don't believe it. Of course, God is in control of the overall course of history. He has all power and He can do whatever He wants to, whenever He wants. It is correct to say that God is "in charge." He watches. He cares. However, God is not controlling every detail of our lives.

People who say that God is in control of all things are implying that He is responsible for all the bad things which happen. You see, if God is in control, then He is the One killing babies. He is spreading sicknesses. He is causing war. Right this instant, someone is in pain, and if God is in control, then He is the One causing that pain. If God is in control, then He is responsible.

Please, don't blame God.

The statement, "God is in control," is a cliché which has been spoken countless times, but it is nowhere in the Bible. In fact, the Bible clearly teaches us that God is not in control of all the terrible things that happen in this world. Let me explain.

Jesus taught us to pray:

> *"Thy kingdom come.*
> *Thy will be done,*

> *On earth as it is in heaven."* (Matt. 6:10)

We are instructed to pray that God's will shall be done on Earth. Why should we pray this? Because right now, God's will is not being done on Earth. Some things are out of control.

God has the authority and power to do whatever He wants, whenever He wants. However, He is not forcing His will upon us. He could if He wanted to, but in the present time His relationship with the world is one of *selective involvement*. At times He intervenes. At times we witness Him answering our prayers. However, He sovereignly has decided *not* to control all things.

So from where does all of the pain and suffering in this world come? There are many sources.

First, we live in a world where bad things happen. God set this world into motion, and it is functioning according to His natural laws. He is not controlling every minute action and reaction. He is watching. He knows what we experience. He wants to help us and He will intervene at times. Yet, we still live in a world where bad things sometimes happen.

It is also true that God has established in this world a law based upon the free will of people:

> *...what a man sows, this he will also reap.*
> (Gal. 6:7)

This verse speaks powerfully to the condition of many people directly reaping the consequences of their own actions, and indirectly when others—often innocents—reap the consequences of the actions of others.

A woman who spends her life chain-smoking very well may spend her last years battling lung cancer. A sexually promiscuous man may catch a venereal disease and suffer unto his death.

On the other hand, an African child with a distended belly knows nothing of global politics, but the barbaric ruler who took the foreign aid intended for food and diverted it to his personal palace has charted that child's course for the future.

It is a very real world out there, and much of our suffering is brought on by choices, either ours or others. Sadly, it is sometimes our ignorance or the ignorance of others we trusted that is at the root.

We also have a spiritual enemy. Jesus taught that there is a real devil in the world, and he is at work killing and destroying people.

Many things happens outside of the will of God. People are suffering. God is not the One causing all that pain. In fact, He wishes such terrible things were not happening to the precious people He loves.

Concerning my sweet mother-in-law who suffered for so many years, I never saw God heal her. She died in pain. Actually that was a relief. That is when God took control. He did not kill her, but He did take her into His arms on that glorious day.

Chapter 5
In the Beginning

Your understanding of the world, suffering, and pain is influenced profoundly by how you envision God's original Creation. God declared that everything He created was 'Good!" (Gen. 1:31) In what way was it good?

When most church-going people think of the Garden of Eden, they envision Adam and Eve strolling through flowers, casually plucking fruit from nearby trees. They picture Eden as a place of leisure and peace, with no suffering nor pain.

That view is wrong in several ways.

First of all, Adam and Eve were placed in the Garden to *work* (Gen. 2:15). Plants did not grow in straight rows by themselves. Weeds did not stay out of the paths on their own accord. The Garden was blessed, but Adam and Eve had to work six days each week to manage it effectively.

When God declared that Creation was good, what did He mean?

I have a woodworking shop that is "Good!" I love to go there on my days off and work on projects. In that shop there are saws, drills, and other tools that make the work easier. One of the good things about my shop is that my youngest son also likes to build things there. When he was younger, I taught him how to use some of the power tools. Occasionally, he still comes to ask my advice on some project of his. I like that. In fact, the shop has been a wonderful place for him and me to build our relationship.

In one sense, the world is similar to my shop. Creation, as originally designed by God, was good in the sense of it being a perfect place for people to live, work, and develop a relationship with God. Identifying this purpose for Creation is key—it is for relationship.

The apostle Paul explained this when he taught the Greek leaders about the true God, saying:

> *...and He made from one, every nation of mankind to live on the face of the earth...that they should seek God, if perhaps they might grope for Him and find Him....* (Acts 17:26-27)

God wants us to seek Him. If necessary, grope for Him. Hence, He placed us in a world in which we need help. We cannot be successful here without Him. We live in a big world, an unfinished world, a world that needs to be managed, a world where bad things sometimes happen. This is a world which needs us and God working together. That is the type of world God created.

Of course, this world has gotten worse because of humanity's sin. Outside of the Garden of Eden, things were and are much more difficult than within it. The world is not a big pillow upon which people are to spend their lives sleeping and causally eating. It needs to be managed. People need to work six days a week. They only can be successful by working with God's aid. They need God. There are difficult and even dangerous things which can cause us to grope for Him. This world is *good* in the sense that it is the perfect environment to fulfill God's purpose—that is, to lead people into a relationship with Him.

Chapter 6
It Is About Relationship

If you think life is about how blessed and happy everyone is, then you may be thrown into confusion when you see someone experiencing serious pain.

Of course, God does not like to see people suffer. He wants to bless everyone. However, blessing us is not His highest priority. Number one is relationship. He wants us to know Him.

Some people will come to know God through the blessings in their lives. They will recognize the goodness they experience as flowing from the One and only Creator.

Others will take the blessings of life for granted or give full credit to their own labors and wisdom. These will go through life never understanding why they exist, and they will miss out on the most fundamental truth of life—that God **is** and that He is the Giver of all that is good (Heb. 11:6; James 1:17). Without this understanding, life is ultimately meaningless.

Yet, these same individuals may discover God in the midst of trials.

I have seen this thousands of times. In my work I travel the world over, and I have stayed in hundreds of homes. Person after person has shared with me the troubles each has experienced—and how in the midst of those trials each reached out to God. When they found themselves helpless and without anyone to whom they could turn, they cried out to God and found Him. Though they suffered at the time, they now realize how the trials that they faced pressed them over the threshold to where their Creator was waiting.

God is not asking for constant attention 24 hours a day, seven days a week. But He does want one's whole attention and affection from time to time. He wants to be loved with a whole heart.

Typically, people do not even know when they are giving only a portion of their hearts to other individuals. They may think they are "tuned in," but frequently they are distracted, their minds are racing with thoughts, and they are eager for the other persons to quit talking so they can share their own ideas or go about their business. He/she rarely makes true heart-to-heart contact with another person.

It is frustrating to be ignored. There is one lady whom I telephone from time to time, and she answers the phone while she is working on her computer. She is very efficient and able to handle multiple tasks. However, talking to her is sometimes frustrating because I cannot get her full attention.

God wants our undivided attention and affection.

Only if you understand this, can you make sense out of life. It is about relationship. God wants us to seek Him and find Him.

God wants you.

Look at the world around you through this lens and everything will appear differently. Life will make more sense.

Chapter 7
An Appointment with Death?

Some people think that God has predestined the length of every person's life—including the day of one's birth and the day of one's death.

In reality, some people die before God wants them to die. Some people commit suicide; that is not God's will. He did not predestine the days of their deaths. Of course, God could have intervened and spared them from a premature death. He has the power and authority to do that. But God has chosen *not* to control everything in this world.

The idea that God controls the day of every person's death often comes from a misunderstanding of certain Bible passages. For example, King David wrote a Psalm to God saying:

> *Thine eyes have seen my unformed substance;*
> *And in Thy book they were written,*
> *The days that were ordained for me,*
> *When as yet there was not one of them.* (Psalm 139:16)

From this Bible verse, some people conclude that God assigns the day of birth and death for every human being and that no one can change the date that he or she is appointed to die.

That is not true. It is wrong to take a Bible verse in which David was talking about his own life and apply it to every human being who ever lived. It is true that God raised King David for a specific purpose at a specific time in history in order to accomplish His plan. However, that gives us no basis to say that the life of every human being has been so tightly orchestrated.

John the Baptist was sent by God to announce the coming of Jesus. Therefore, John was born in the same region of the world and at the same time that Jesus was. It is reasonable to think that God orchestrated this.

Indeed, God may have ordained certain individuals such as John the Baptist and David to live on the Earth and fulfill a specific destiny during a set time period. However, there is no verse in the Bible which says every human being has an exact appointed day to be born and a day to die.

To a great extent, our own life is in our own hands. How we live, what we eat, and how fast we drive our cars play a part in determining how long we live.

Sometimes our lives may be in the hands of others. On the hospital operating table, our lives may be in a doctor's hands. In war, the soldier's life may be in an enemy's hands. When a bomb comes into the hands of a terrorist, then the lives of thousands may be cut short by a person living in opposition to God.

Chapter 8
Why Do Babies Die?

A mother who has a baby who dies is left with a haunting question: Why did a loving and good God take her innocent child?

If we look at life the way the Bible teaches us to view it, we will have many possible answers. The death of the baby may have been the result of:

1. an accident
2. improper nutrition
3. suffocation or poisoning
4. the random selection of genes leading to a genetic disorder
5. an infection, virus, or disease
6. Sudden Infant Death Syndrome
7. a medical problem which we do not understand
8. murder
9. the activity of the devil
10. God

Any one or combination of the above explanations may be possible, along with an unlimited number of other explanations.

I hesitate in listing number ten, because I do not want people to credit God with the killing of children. God is good and I never would tell a mother that God killed her baby. However, if we are going to be true to what the Bible tells us, then we must include this as one possibility. The Bible tells us that after King David committed adultery with Bathsheba, "the Lord struck the child" and "the child died" (II Sam. 12:15-18). In some cases, God may be responsible for a child's death.

It is worth noting that God took King David's baby into heaven. After David mourned the death of his child, he told his servants that his child would not come back to life, but someday he would see his child again (II Sam. 12:18-23). It is reassuring that even this child who was born of an adulterous affair was welcomed into the presence of God.

Though we must admit that God, in some rare cases, can take a child home, the most relevant answer that should be given to a mother who has lost a child is that we live in a world where tragedies happen. Things are out of control. We have not yet learned to effectively manage all disease, nutrition, genetic, and medical problems. Bad stuff happens. That is why the baby died.

Chapter 9
Living Creatures Suffer

For the last few years, my wife and I have had several pets, including two dogs. When our older dog died, the younger one wandered aimlessly around our home for days. She was mourning the death of her long-time companion. Interestingly, she wanted to stay close beside us. She would follow us from room to room and lie at our feet whenever we sat. She wanted our presence during that time of loneliness.

We also raise exotic birds. Behind our countryside home, we have a pen with doves, pheasants, and peacocks. An emu also walks around our two-acre pasture. If you aren't familiar with this bird, think of an ostrich, for, indeed, this is a close relative, but about three-quarters the size of its larger cousin.

Emus don't like change. If you change their environment or scare them in any significant way, they may stop eating for two or three weeks. They walk around in a daze, trying to make sense of life again. Hence their cousins, the ostriches, deserve their reputation of sticking their heads in the sand to hide from danger and things which they do not understand.

As with some animals, people often go into a daze when they experience tragedy. If a loved one has died, they need to mourn. While they are trying to make sense out of life, they usually want someone close.

When their minds are confused, their hearts long to be filled. For people, the confusion resulting from tragedy usually stems back to the question, "Why? Why did this happen?"

No one really can answer this question for them, because his/her entire sense of security has been shaken. Simple words will not put their lives back together. At best, we can offer a missing piece here and there while they reassemble their own thought processes. And we can be there. Our presence is important.

Some of the most godly people I know have had their faith shattered by tragedy. One friend of mine held his daughter and watched her die as she was lying pinned under an automobile. I don't know how he survived that experience. I don't know how anyone survives the death of a child. How do they get up in the morning? How do they ever go back to work?

Some people lose their faith in God. At least they think they have lost it. The confusion in their minds creates a smoke screen between them and the God Whom they once trusted. Yet faith is anchored in the heart, not the head. When I probe beneath the confusion, I find their hearts still flickering with a light.

Perhaps this is your present relationship with God. You may not understand Him, but you still long for Him. That longing is evidence of a seed—a seed of faith still rooted deep within you. Given enough time and nurturing, that seed will grow, reaching into your mind where thoughts can be realigned, eventually to form a garden of truth again.

Chapter 10 Some Tragedies Work Out for Good

Have you ever watched someone whom you love suffer? It hurts. You want to help them. From where do such feelings come? Why do we feel compassion for others?

You and I are created in God's image. We are like Him. That is why we experience feelings of compassion.

God does not want us to suffer. Nor does He want us to be alone in what suffering we do experience. God has given us much freedom to live, work, and make decisions in this world, but He desires to be with us and to help us.

When we turn to Him for help, He will respond. The Bible explains that God wants us to seek Him and find Him. We also are assured that God is "not far from each one of us" (Acts 17:27). He is present. He is within the distance of your next breath. He hears your sighs. Furthermore, the Bible promises us that if we draw near to Him, then He will draw near to us.

It does not matter what circumstances in which we find ourselves, what mistakes we have made, or what tragedies have happened, God is there with open arms to accept us. If we come to Him, He will welcome us.

He also will turn the difficulties and trials of our

lives into more positive outcomes. Paul the Apostle explained this, saying:

> *And we know that God causes all things to work together for good to those who love God, to those who are called according to His purpose.* (Rom. 8:28)

Let me give you an example of God turning a tragedy around for good. You may remember reading on the front pages of many newspapers about the shootings and killings that took place in several high schools in North America. In one school in Canada, a student died who was the son of an Anglican priest. This was a random act, a tragic murder. No reason. A useless end of life. It was time for a minister and his wife to live out their faith.

And they did. Three years after the tragedy, I sat across the table from them, and I saw in their eyes both pain and love. They suffered, but they were able to forgive the young man who killed their son. Today they raise their remaining children, but they also travel across Canada speaking to youth in schools. Tens of thousands of young people have heard their story. It has stirred many to forgive others of the wrongs they have experienced. The death of their son has been a window for multitudes to see into the heart of God.

Most tragedies do not turn into such obvious and public demonstrations of good. But God will intervene. He will work things out for good—somehow, some way. He will be glorified in every situation and every situation will be turned around for good, if we bring our lives into alignment with the will of God.

Consider King David. Earlier I mentioned how he committed adultery with Bathsheba and the child born from that relationship died. David was devastated, but after he mourned the death, he brought his life back into alignment with the will of God. Among other things, he took responsibility and married Bathsheba. They had another child, Solomon, who grew up to establish peace and prosperity for the nation of Israel, and to this day is still recognized as the wisest man who ever lived.

God causes all things to work for good on behalf of those who love Him and are called according to His purpose (Rom. 8:28). On the other hand, the Bible gives us no assurance that all things will work out for good if we do not find a place of peace and solace in Him.

Chapter 11
Rich in Faith

I have walked through regions of the world where poverty is crushing. Yet there I have met some of the happiest people on Earth.

In one remote region of the Philippines, I saw some children in a fishing village laughing as they played with sticks and a ball. They caught my attention, so I walked over to share in their enthusiasm. I saw that the "ball" which they hit back and forth was a dead rat. How strange it seemed that they thought nothing of their lack, when many children in my home country would feel deprived if they did not have the latest and the best athletic equipment.

On another occasion, I watched a group of Filipino men play a game of basketball. They dribbled a well-worn ball across packed, dusty soil, and lobbed the ball into a rusty hoop hanging from a leaning wood post. The area was alive with activity, competition, and focus. I was caught in the energy of the moment. Soon I noticed that some of the ball players had no shoes. A few others played with one shoe. They only owned one shoe, so that is what they wore.

Most of my friends in North America have a closet full of shoes, yet they are no happier than most of the people I have met in developing nations. In my home country, people do not experience the same hunger, diseases, and wars, but they are, generally speaking, no happier.

I found reality to the Bible words: God has chosen the poor to be rich in faith (James 2:5). This has many implications, but one of the most obvious is how disadvantaged people in developing nations seem to have simple faith. If they have discovered a relationship with God, they hold to it as a child holds to its parents. They trust. Even in the most difficult circumstances, they are able to keep their hearts oriented toward God.

The words of Jesus have helped me understand this. The Lord said:

> *"The lamp of the body is the eye; if therefore your eye is clear, your whole body will be full of light. But if your eye is bad, your whole body will be full of darkness."*
> (Matt. 6:22-23a)

The "eye" of which Jesus is speaking is not just the physical organ located in your head. There is a deeper meaning. He is speaking of the focus of your thoughts and heart—the orientation of your faith and life. If your orientation is right, then you will be filled with light, that is, the life and energy of God.

Jesus goes on to teach the proper orientation. He told His listeners to look at the birds of the air and the lilies of the field (Matt. 6:26-30). He explained that God takes care of the birds, so certainly He will take take of us. God arrays the flowers with beauty and He cares much more for us than He does for them. Jesus was exhorting us to look at the goodness of God. That is the proper orientation of our lives. If our "eyes" are set on that, then we will be full of life.

I have discovered this principle to be true, no matter where people live or what they experience. I do not want to minimize the pain and suffering through which people go. Yet, I have observed how the quality of people's lives is primarily determined—*not* by the trials they face—but by their ability to focus or refocus on the goodness of God.

The Psalm-writer gives us an excellent example of this, which I will share with you in the next chapter.

Chapter 12
But God Is Good

The writer of Psalms 73 speaks of a time in his life when his focus moved away from the goodness of God and onto the trials which he was facing.

He began this Psalm by saying:

Surely God is good.... (Psalm 73:1)

This is the right perspective. He was looking at the birds of the air and the lilies of the field. He was conscious of God's love, provisions, and care.

The Psalm-writer continues, but his focus shifts from the goodness of God to his own struggles. The specific trial with which he was dealing at the time was a lack of finances. What made it worse was that he began noticing that many other people were prospering, and the people who seemed to be the richest were those who were not serving God. Corrupt people seemed to have the best of life!

With his mind fixed on injustice, his thoughts spiraled downward into a dark pit:

Behold, these are the wicked;
And always at ease, they have increased
in wealth.
Surely in vain I have kept my heart pure,
And washed my hands in innocence;

For I have been stricken all day long,
And chastened every morning.
(Psalm 73:12-14)

Serving God seemed useless. God was not rewarding him for his labors. Mired down in self-pity, the Psalm-writer concluded: "Life is not fair!"

We all come to this conclusion at some point in our lives. Life isn't fair. Some of us face trials far greater than others around us. Some people suffer in pain for years. Others watch loved ones die. There are thousands of children born with serious genetic defects. Many people experience tragic divorces. Others go through bankruptcy and financial devastation. Some people have chemical imbalances that cause mental anguish every day of their lives. Others live consumed in loneliness, fear, shame, and rejection.

It is obvious: life isn't fair. The sooner you face this fact, the sooner you will be able to deal with the trials and the unfairness of life with which you have to cope.

Once you admit that life is not fair, you can go on to make another—a separate—observation: that God is good. Please see these as two distinct truths.

Life is not fair, but God is good.

Until you recognize these as two distinct facts, you will not be able to keep the proper orientation of your mind and heart. If you confuse the nature of the world with the nature of God, sooner or later you will find yourself in the pit at the bottom of a downward spiral of negative thoughts.

This is what the writer of the Psalm went on to

explain. After hitting bottom, he came to his senses and took on a different perspective:

When I pondered to understand this,
It was troublesome in my sight
Until I came into the sanctuary of God....
(Psalm 73:16-17)

Indeed, the unfairness of life is hard to understand. It only makes sense from the perspective of God and His final authority over this world.

From that perspective, the writer reminded himself that God does not always administer justice immediately, but He does judge righteously and ultimately. Sooner or later the wicked reap what they have sown. Destruction comes upon their lives (Psalm 73:18-20). Ultimately, God will judge every person according to their deeds (Rom. 2:6-8).

The writer then realized how short-sighted and distorted his perception had been when he had been focusing on the wicked and their prosperity:

When my heart was embittered,
And I was pierced within,
Then I was senseless and ignorant;
I was like a beast before Thee.
(Psalm 73:21-22)

He admitted to and confessed his anger. He realized that he had been thinking as a beast.

As he came into the sanctuary, he began to see again the goodness of God. He reminded himself of the eternity of joy which was in his future. From the perspective of eternity, life's trials began to fade.

But he also became conscious of the greatest blessing which he experienced while on this Earth. He remembered how God had taken hold of his right hand and faithfully guided him through life (Psalm 73:23-24). Most importantly, he realized how he had experienced God's presence, acceptance, and love:

> *Whom have I in heaven but Thee?*
> *And besides Thee, I desire nothing on earth.*
> *My flesh and my heart may fail,*
> *But God is the strength of my heart and my portion forever...*
> *But as for me, the nearness of God is my good;*
> *I have made the Lord God my refuge,*
> *That I may tell of all Thy works.*
> (Psalm 73:25-28)

He made it. He found peace and victory. In the midst of his trials, he brought his mind and heart to rest in God.

Chapter 13
Why Did Job Have to Suffer?

Many people have never experienced the nearness of God. They cannot understand how someone could be so captivated by the love of God that they would sing a love song to Him. Others have tasted of His presence, but lost or forgotten the flavor. There are also those who know it, treasure it, and can't imagine living without it.

There are even people who are very religious, but never have experienced the nearness of God. They live a good life. They believe in God. They even pray. But they never have experienced God's presence.

Job was like this. The Bible tells us that he was a righteous man, fearing God. Yet, he suffered terribly and came out of it knowing God more intimately. Allow me to explain.

In only one day, Job lost his children, servants, and livestock (Job 1:13-19). Then Job was struck from head to toe with boils that caused him intense pain (Job 2:7-13). So terrible was his suffering that he despaired of life and wished he never had been born:

> *"Let the day perish on which I was to be born,*
> *And the night which said, 'A boy is conceived.'*
> *May that day be darkness...."* (Job 3:3-4)

In this classic work of poetic art, we read about three of Job's friends who came to his side to give him counsel. His counselors basically told him that he must have done something wrong, he must have sinned, he must have offended God for such terrible things to befall him. In response, Job repeatedly denied it and said that he knew of no sin in his life deserving of such punishment.

In the midst of Job's suffering and confusion, he cried out to God: "Why?" When he received no answer and he could make no sense of the pain he was experiencing, he began to demand God give him an answer:

> *"I will give full vent to my complaint;*
> *I will speak in the bitterness of my soul.*
> *I will say to God, 'Do not condemn me;*
> *Let me know why Thou dost contend with*
> *me.'"* (Job 10:1b-2)

Job became very angry and accused God of wrongdoing:

> *"Know that God has wronged me,*
> *And closed His net around me.*
> *Behold, I cry, 'Violence!' but I get no*
> *answer;*
> *I shout for help, but there is no justice."*
> (Job 19:6-7)

After Job and his three friends finally ended their discussion and debate, a young man named Elihu spoke up with the true answers from God. Elihu rightly revealed that Job was not being punished for any sin he had committed. In fact, the entire issue of "Why?" missed the point. Elihu harshly rebuked Job, and he identified the real issue when he said:

> *"Why do you complain against Him,*
> *That He does not give an account of all*
> *His doings?"* (Job 33:13)

The real issue, Elihu declared, was that Job was reacting to his suffering wrongly:

> *" 'Job ought to be tried to the limit,*
> *Because he answers like wicked men...*
> *He multiplies his words against God.' "*
> (Job 34:36-37)

Job had the audacity to demand God to give an answer for why He was allowing such suffering.

After Elihu made his case that God owes no one an answer for anything He does, God Himself spoke from heaven and rebuked Job, saying:

> *"Where were you when I laid the foundation of the earth?...."* (Job 38:4)

God went on declaring His own greatness, and in comparison, the smallness of humanity (chapters 38-41). By the time God was done, Job was humbled and had only one thing to say:

"...I have declared that which I did not understand,
Things too wonderful for me, which I did not know...
I have heard of Thee by the hearing of the ear;
But now my eye sees Thee;
Therefore I retract,
And I repent in dust and ashes."

(Job 42:3-6)

By the end of the book of Job, the observant reader understands that God did not cause Job's sufferings, but He orchestrated the events of Job's life to get his attention. God revealed Himself to Job.

Consider again what Job finally realized:

"I have heard of Thee by the hearing of the ear;
But now my eye sees Thee." (Job 42:5)

Job had believed in God and heard about Him all of his life. Job had even lived his life in obedience to the will of God. But it was not until the end of his period of suffering that he could say, "Now my eye sees Thee!"

Please consider how profound this is: God is God; He owes no one an explanation for anything He does or allows to happen. To realize this is to bow before Him. From that position, He can be seen more clearly. And seeing Him is the single most important accomplishment in any person's life.

Chapter 14
I Was Angry at God

And seeing Him is the single most important accomplishment in any person's life.

I never have suffered as Job did, but I went through a major period of disillusionment which changed my life. I invested everything—not just money, but my heart and soul—to do what I believed God wanted me to do. After four years of doing my absolute best, everything fell apart. My wife and I were unable to make a payment on our house for several months. One of our two cars was repossessed. There was no food in the kitchen and we had three little children for whom to care. The stress on our marriage was tremendous. My wife says that the hardest time was not when we had no food, but when we had no toilet paper in the house!

I fell into depression. I couldn't get myself out of it. Worst of all, I didn't want to. I was angry at God. I was not conscious of my anger, but deep inside I felt that He had let me down. He had failed me...after I had done my best to live for Him.

At the bottom of my confusion, a crisis moment came. I had been mentoring two young men to whom I will refer as Stu and Greg. They wanted to serve God with all of their hearts, and I was honored to know them. They looked to me for guidance in various areas of Christian living. We prayed together a lot. It was a time in our lives when we thought that if we just prayed enough, if we just had enough faith, then God would do anything for us.

We were bonded in heart. One day Stu gave me his favorite coat, an expensive white coat, a coat that signified who he was. He wanted me to have his precious possession, and I wore it with satisfaction.

A short time later, Stu went on a vacation with his wife and two young children. On the way home they were in a tragic car wreck. Stu fell asleep at the wheel. His children and wife came through with minor injuries, but Stu was killed.

When Greg contacted me to let me know what had happened, I was stunned. It couldn't happen. It was not right. Stu was in his twenties and just beginning his life's work and family. God would not allow this to happen!

Greg was just as upset as I was. We would not accept the death of our friend. We could not. This could not be God's will, so Greg decided to go to the funeral parlor, yank Stu out of the coffin, and tell him to come back to life. I didn't go with him, but I contacted the widow and explained how we were praying.

At the funeral parlor, Stu did not come back to life. Greg couldn't do it. God wouldn't do it. I cried. I cried a lot.

My life took a new direction that day. I realized that I can't force God to do what I want Him to do. What made it real was Stu's body. You see, in the car wreck, a pole had come through the windshield of the vehicle and taken off a portion of his head. It was too much. It was too real. I knew that we couldn't raise our friend from the dead.

Today, more than 12 years later, the coat Stu gave me still hangs in my closet. I don't wear it. But I haven't been able to throw it away.

Through that difficult time of my life, I learned something about God. I can't force Him to do what I want Him to do. He is too big. I can't twist His arm. I learned something else about Him but I can't put it into words. I just know better Who He is because He touched me.

Chapter 15
Healing Hobbies

I have been so fortunate. I am physically healthy. My wife and I love each other. Our children are happy. We have enough money. My work is fun. I get to travel and write books that help people. My life is filled with meaning and purpose.

Of course, it would be nice if I still could grow hair on top of my head, but other than that, life is basically good.

Things could have gone differently. There were many opportunities when a slight change in events would have sent my life down a tragic road, or when the tragedies that have happened could have left me in a pit. I especially am fearful of the pit, because I have watched myself fall into self-pity and anger toward God during several trying periods of my life.

I am sure you know this, but the pit isn't fun. For the first few years of my marriage, I would pull my wife into the pit with me. She won't join me there anymore. She always finds something—anything—better to do. It is lonely in the pit because no one wants to join me.

I find it easiest to get out of the pit by doing things I enjoy. I like to mow my lawn. I love to drive my riding lawn mower because I feel as though I am accomplishing something without having to think too hard. I also love my woodworking shop. There is something wonderful about cutting a piece of wood and getting sawdust all over my face. It makes me feel as if I am a different person.

I also like to clean my shop. That may sound strange, but I think it is because of my father; when I was growing up I often had to clean his woodshop. After I did a good job, Dad was always pleased with me. I think, even today, I still feel I'm a good person if I have a clean shop. So no matter what is happening in my life—even if everything is crashing in—I feel pretty good so long as my shop is clean.

I suppose these activities are much the same as looking at the birds of the air and the lilies of the field. They change the focus of my life. I sense God on the other side of these simple blessings.

It reminds me of the children in the Philippines. They taught me how to catch a huge beetle (about three inches long) that is native to that region of the world. What is cool is that the beetle is so big you can tie a string or a long piece of hair around its neck and pretend that it is your dog on a leash. You still can do that, even if you don't have shoes, or enough food, or a mother.

Chapter 16
The Nearness of God

One of the reasons I travel to difficult places in the world is because I find God's presence there. Not only is the work personally rewarding, but God abides in the whole-hearted contact of one person with another.

People in developing nations also reveal their hearts when they sing. They don't have expensive instruments, and their music never will be on CDs, but it flows through my spirit everyday. In many of the villages I visit, the only musical instruments they have are drums made of hollow logs and stretched animal skins. I also have seen many tin cans filled with gravel and used as shakers to keep rhythm.

I like listening in the morning before the sun rises. I love the sound of roosters crowing outside my bamboo or mud hut. I like to hear a pig squealing off in the distance. And then when someone in a nearby hut rises early to sing to God, I like to lie motionless on my wooden bed and listen. It is as rain splashing on a still pond. It is as my wife's breath as she drifts asleep in my arms. It feels as if someone nearby is kissing God.

I don't deserve the goodness of God which I have experienced, but I surely am grateful for what I have been able to taste.

Sometimes God feels far away. Years ago when I was disillusioned and angry at God, He seemed to have abandoned me totally. Actually I didn't want Him around then. Eventually I had to forgive Him. Imagine that: *little me* forgave God—the Creator of the universe. I was bitter in my heart and I judged Him as the guilty one.

I also asked Him to forgive me for thinking that He was the bully; forgive me for accusing Him of doing terrible things. We made up.

I have learned that my anger toward people also can steal from me the nearness of God. It seems especially important that I do not hold judgments against those who are supposed to be closest to my heart, such as my parents, wife, and children. Peter wrote in the Bible how a husband must honor his wife, or his prayers will be hindered (I Peter 3:7). I do not think God really is moving away to a different location, but somehow He does seem to be inaccessible when I have walls in my heart separating me from the people whom I should be loving.

Through the years I also have learned that when I get angry at the Church, I am hindered from experiencing the nearness of God. If you ever have been involved in a church community, you know that relationships can get complicated and people can get hurt. Often their pain is understandable. However, the resulting judgments rob the one who hardens his or her heart. John explained in the Bible that if anyone hates the family of God, God's light becomes shadowed to them (I John 2:11).

I have to admit that I have had many opportunities to get angry at Church people. Sadly, a few of those opportunities I accepted. At the time I did not know that I was traveling down the path of isolation. I felt totally justified in noticing how others had done stupid or even mean things. I simply was protecting myself and deciding not to expose my heart to the future possibilities of getting hurt.

Sooner or later I would notice that God seemed just as distant as the people from whom I was estranged. When I finally got lonely or feeling as if I were carrying on with life's labors all on my own, I started to wonder why God seemed aloof. Each time I have asked God to show me why, He has answered. It takes time for the light to dawn, but sooner or later I see the wall in my own heart...which I erected against some other person or group of people whom I should be loving.

When I forgive people and God, He reveals Himself to me. Again, I experience His nearness.

I hope I never forget this. I hope I remember to forgive the next time God feels far away. He is so good and I don't want to offend Him. I don't like to be without Him and I cherish His nearness.

Chapter 17
Why, God, Why?

In the beginning of this book, I said that I would address the fundamental question "Why, God, why?" And I hope that I have done this. I have discussed the fact that suffering is real and painful, and that God would not have any of us suffer, but that He has chosen to not control everything. There is randomness in this world—it is by God's design. People have free will, and again, that is by God's design. Finally, there is evil and chaos in this world, and while that is not by God's design, it is a reality of the world in which we now live and is the reason we pray:

> *"Thy Kingdom come.*
> *Thy will be done,*
> *On earth as it is in heaven...."*
>
> (Matt. 6:10)

Further, I have said that while the world is unfair, God is good. I have attempted to draw a line in your mind to understand that the unfairness and tragedy of this world is not a reflection of God, but God's goodness is intended to lead us through our present difficulties. Indeed, God can turn any tragedy for good. God also can use tragedy to turn us to Him. It is through the difficult circumstances in our lives that we strive to reach Him in new and vital ways. Indeed, this is the crux of suffering, its final work—either for good or evil—and the choice is ours to make.

God does not control all that happens to us, but He destines what becomes of it if we allow Him to do so. When life, or our actions, or the actions of those we trust, or the son of evil himself throws such calamity at us that we no longer can stand, we have to make a choice: give in to the ultimate thrust of such difficulty and accept that God Himself is evil (as we attribute all things to Him), or accept that while life is unfair, God is good.

If we accept that God is good, we realize something about God that we never knew before. We peer into the depths of His goodness. We learn about the power of His love. We partake of the invincibility of His Spirit, and we pass this on to others.

And herein lies the victory: that while suffering, pain, and destruction would have made us alienated from God and blaming Him by virtue of His apparent alienation from us, God's goodness makes us stronger in the very arena in which we once were weak. Our hearts grow strong, our minds firm, our emotions rich and steady, and we set to work spreading this news that God is good. Our very weakness, our vulnerability, our naiveté, become the strength which God uses to help others. We become overcomers.

We may never leave our wheel chairs, we may never fully emerge from our depression, we may never regain use of maimed hands and limbs, and lost children may never be seen this side of heaven, but God's goodness advances into a world which desperately needs Him. It advances through previous suffering—it advances through our renewal.

Oh that God would raise every one of us, feed and fill every one of us. Some believe that He will, and I would not stand in the way of any who would seek the miraculous intervention of the God Who heals. But for as many as receive this touch now in this present life, there are many, as my dear mother-in-law, for whom the touch of God is reserved for a later time. And the provision offered these wayfarers in this sometimes-inhospitable land is simply His goodness, His mysterious, yet fulfilling, life-changing goodness.

Chapter 18
The Answer

I will end this book telling you about a child, a beautiful boy, who once stood next to me while I taught in an African village. I was teaching the people about Jesus, that He had died for them and now God desires to forgive them of their sins. Many of the people were hearing this message for the first time. They honored me. They looked to me as if I had come from a great and distant land to bring them the news which even their ancestors had longed to hear.

But the child, maybe three years old, caressed a nearby pole which supported the canvas roof under which we gathered. No clothes. No shoes. Eyes and nose that needed a mother to wipe. That child did not understand what I was saying.

Thinking of that child channels thoughts down two distinct pathways in my mind.

The first path is down a rollercoaster where questions flash past me: "Why, God, why? Why do You allow this? Why don't You do something? Can't You help? What kind of God are You? Are You there? Don't You care? I don't understand. This is too hard."

On the other hand, if I stop the rollercoaster before cresting the hill, I can see from a higher perspective. Then a gentle breeze brings a different stream of thoughts through my mind.

Realizing that God placed us in a world where people reap the consequences of their own actions, I look for a cause: "Did the father of this child abandon him? Did the mother die? Or was she simply unable to care for another? Was it war or AIDS that left this child without a home? Has the government diverted funds intended for his care and feeding? Do people in my country know about this child? What can I do for him?"

Then it hits me. Where did this compassion in my own heart originate? Doesn't God have to be the Source? If I even can ask these questions, is that not evidence that I must be a part of the solution? When I feed the poor, comfort the sick, shelter the homeless, direct the lost, love the unlovely—what manner of person do I become? How does it change me?

Who did God leave on the Earth beside me—beside us? What was Adam's commission from the very beginning? Was it not to replenish the Earth and subdue it, cultivate it, and finish it? That commission has not changed, in spite of the facts that humanity has sinned, the garden was repossessed, his wife was corrupted, his children were alienated, and his work was made miserable by thorns.

Now, if I am changed by the good that I do, what manner of person would I become if God were to intervene without my involvement each and every time there was a crisis? What would become of my character if I didn't learn that for my every action—my every choice—there was a reaction, a reaping, a sowing? What if I lived free of this law? What would become of my character...

- if nations were free to rape, rob, and kill, and yet no child burned?
- if callous men held God in disregard and those beneath them prospered above all the Earth?
- if the innocent and the loving perished under the heel of the oppressor and no blood trail was found, no cry heard?
- if solutions to calamities magically appeared with no effort from people?

What do people become when they no longer see suffering, no longer feel it, and thus become immune to it?

What we see in a suffering world is humanity's work, not God's. And we recognize a choice...to turn to the needs and help, or turn away and grow callous ourselves, becoming a part of the nightmare rather than the dream.

Our choices come loudly to our faces. We cannot call ourselves godly people and at the same time ignore their shrieking. Their tears are sent to remind us, their cries to call us, their pain to convert us, their lives to teach us, their deaths to propel us.

When a small child is left homeless and our hearts cry out to God: "Why?" the answer that might come is: "Help him." When crops fail and leaders fail and economies collapse, taking whole nations of innocent victims with them, and our hearts cry: "God, why?" the answer might come again: "Help them."

When the multitude faced hunger for lack of food and the disciples brought the problem to Jesus, His answer was: "Feed them."

God's answers to our questions are not intended to solve all our problems—God forbid. Pray that He never quenches the fire, never fully satisfies the thirst, never fully addresses the questions posed to Him by unsatisfied hearts. But pray that His answers impart wisdom and that His power comes as a result of our hearts' cries.

You may not hear the answer you want when you go to God with your grievance. Instead, you may receive a call, a direction, a grace to do something you never have done before. Your questions may serve only to qualify you for a higher level of service, and yes, of understanding. And your answer back to Him may determine what He does in this world.

Books That Will Change Your Life
by Harold R. Eberle

TWO BECOME ONE (Second edition)

Releasing God's Power for Romance, Sexual Freedom and Blessings in Marriage

Kindle afresh the "buzz of love." Find out how to make God's law of binding forces work for you instead of against you. The keys to a thrilling, passionate, and fulfilling marriage can be yours if you want them. This book is of great benefit to pastors, counselors, young singles, divorcees and especially married people. Couples are encouraged to read it together.

THE COMPLETE WINESKIN (Fourth edition)

The Body of Christ is in a reformation. God is pouring out the Holy Spirit and our wineskins must be changed to handle the new wine. Will the Church come together in unity? Where do small group meetings fit? How does the anointing of God work and what is your role? What is the 5-fold ministry? How are apostles, prophets, evangelists, pastors and teachers going to rise up and work together? This book puts into words what you have been sensing in your spirit. (Eberle's best seller, translated into many languages, distributed worldwide.)

THE LIVING SWORD

"The truth shall set you free." So then why does Christian fight Christian over doctrinal issues that seem so clear to each side? Can both be right, or wrong? Learn how Jesus used the Scriptures in His day and then apply those principles to controversial issues currently facing us such as women in the ministry, divorce and remarriage, prosperity, God's plan for our lives,.... What we need is the leading of the Holy Spirit on these subjects. This book will bring the Scriptures alive and set you free.

GOD'S LEADERS FOR TOMORROW'S WORLD

(Revised/expanded edition) You sense a call to leadership in your life, but questions persist: "Does God want me to rise up? Is this pride? Do I truly know where to lead? How can I influence people?" Through a new understanding of leadership dynamics, learn how to develop godly charisma. Confusion will melt into order when you see the God-ordained lines of authority. Fear of leadership will change to confidence as you learn to handle power struggles. Move into your "metron," that is, your God-given authority. You can be all God created you to be!

PRECIOUS IN HIS SIGHT A Fresh Look at the Nature of Man
During the Fourth Century Augustine taught about the nature of man using as his key Scripture a verse in the book of Romans which had been mistranslated. Since that time the Church has embraced a false concept of man which has negatively influenced every area of Christianity. It is time for Christians to come out of darkness! This book, considered by many to be Harold Eberle's greatest work, has implications upon our understanding of sin, salvation, Who God is, evangelism, the world around us and how we can live the daily, victorious lifestyle.

YOU SHALL RECEIVE POWER
Moving Beyond Pentecostal & Charismatic Theology
God's Spirit will fill you in measures beyond what you are experiencing presently. This is not just about Pentecostal or Charismatic blessings. There is something greater. It is for all Christians, and it will build a bridge between those Christians who speak in tongues and those who do not. It is time for the whole Church to take a fresh look at the work of the Holy Spirit in our individual lives. This book will help you. It will challenge you, broaden your perspective, set you rejoicing, fill you with hope, and leave you longing for more of God.

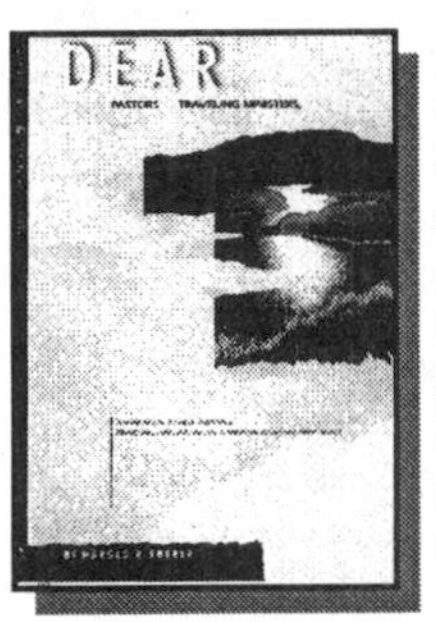

DEAR PASTORS AND TRAVELING MINISTERS,
Here is a manual to help pastors and traveling ministers relate and minister together effectively. Topics are addressed such as ethical concerns, finances, authority, scheduling,.... In addition to dealing with real-life situations, an appendix is included with very practical worksheets to offer traveling ministers and local pastors a means to communicate with each other. Pastors and traveling ministers can make their lives and work much easier by using this simple, yet enlightening, manual.

DEVELOPING A PROSPEROUS SOUL
VOL I: **HOW TO OVERCOME A POVERTY MIND-SET**
VOL II: **HOW TO MOVE INTO GOD'S FINANCIAL BLESSINGS**
There are fundamental changes you can make in the way you think which will help release God's blessings. This is a balanced look at the promises of God with practical steps you can take to move into financial freedom. It is time for Christians to recapture the financial arena.

Spiritual Realities

Here they are—Harold R. Eberle's series explaining how the spiritual world and natural world relate.

Vol I: The Spiritual World and How We Access It

Here is a scriptural foundation for understanding the spiritual world. Learn how to access that world, touch God, and experience His blessings. Be aware of the dangers and false manifestations. Release God's power into your life and the world around us.

Vol II: The Breath of God in Us

A study on the nature and origin of the human spirit, soul, and body. Knowing God's activities within our being. Understanding the spiritual energies which God releases in us to think, be physically healthy, and be sucessful.

Vol. III: Escaping Dualism (Second Edition)

Understand how God created you to live as a whole human being: redeeming the soul, knowing God's will, sanctifying "soul power" and finding freedom as a child of God. This book will set you free!

Vol IV: Powers and Activities of the Human Spirit

God created you in His image, with His breath. Discover what this means in relation to your creative powers, spoken words, dreams, and experiences in space/time. Here is a Biblical explanation of spiritual phenomena.

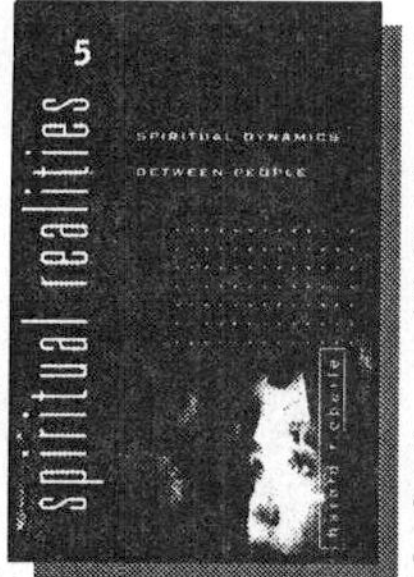

Vol V: Spiritual Dynamics Between People

What is going on spiritually between you and the people around you? Now you can understand spiritual bonds, authority streams, group consciousness, family dynamics, the power of free will and covenants.

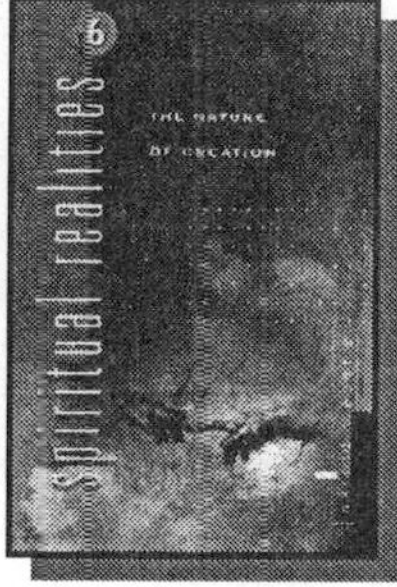

Vol VI: The Nature of Creation

The spiritual and natural worlds overlap. This has profound implications for our understanding of Creation, the origin of life and death, the nature of time, laws governing our universe, how our thoughts influence the natural world, and much more.

Most Recent Releases

Grace...the Power to Reign

The Light Shining from Romans 5-8

We struggle against sin and yearn for God's highest. Yet, on a bad day it is as as if we are fighting with gravity. Questions go unanswered:

- Where is the power to overcome temptations and trials?
- Is God really willing to breathe into us so that these dry bones can live and we may stand strong?

For anyone who ever has clenched his fist in the struggle to live godly, here are the answers. Just as there is a force in the world pushing us to sin, there is a greater force flowing from God which can lift us, transform us, and make us what He wants us to be. It is grace! It is grace which few have grasped, yet, so many have sought desperately. Now you can find it.

Bringing the Future into Focus

An Introduction to the Progressive Christian Worldview

What does the future hold? Will there be peace or war? Are the people of God going to rise up in glory and unity or will they be overcome by apathy and deception? Is Jesus coming for a spotless Bride or is He going to rescue a tattered band of zealots out of a wicked chaotic mess? Where is God taking humanity in the Twenty-First Century?

This book will answer your questions and fill you with hope.

If God is Good, Why is there so much Suffering and Pain?

Life isn't fair! Terrorist bombings. Ethnic cleansing. Body-ravaging diseases. Murder. Child abuse. Natural disasters. Genetic maladies. These travesties, global and seemingly relentless, drive us to the limits of our reasoning. When pain and suffering invade our well-laid plans for a good life, we ask the gut question: Why, God, why? In this book, Harold R. Eberle evaluates the role God plays in the Earth, explores the origin of suffering, and reassures us of God kind intentions toward us.

Worldcast Ministries

A significant portion of the profit from book sales goes to the support of interdenominational Christian missions, Bible colleges, charitable work, and orphanages in developing countries around the world. This work is done through the oversight of Worldcast Ministries, which is an organization overseen by Harold R. Eberle and a staff of volunteer and paid workers. Worldcast Ministries is a ministry based on the belief that God is raising the Church up to a position of unity, maturity, and glory. We believe that the greatest revival the world has ever seen will take place between now and the Second Coming of our Lord Jesus Christ.

If you are looking for something meaningful in which to be involved, we welcome your financial support and we encourage you to join us in helping fulfill the Great Commission to go and make disciples of all nations.